A Touchstone Book

POLICE

WORK

by Leonard Freed

Foreword by Studs Terkel

A TOUCHSTONE BOOK

PUBLISHED BY SIMON AND SCHUSTER, NEW YORK

Books by Leonard Freed

BLACK IN WHITE AMERICA   Grossman, New York, 1969
MADE IN GERMANY   Grossman, New York, 1970
BERLIN   Time-Life Books, New York, 1978

A Touchstone Book
Published by Simon and Schuster
A Division of Gulf & Western Corporation
Simon & Schuster Building
Rockefeller Center
1230 Avenue of the Americas
New York, New York 10020

TOUCHSTONE and colophon are trademarks of Simon & Schuster
Manufactured in the United States of America
Printed by Pollack-Weir Graphics, Inc.
Platemaking by Graphi-Krome Corp.

10 9 8 7 6 5 4 3 2 1

Library of Congress Cataloging in Publication Data

Freed, Leonard.
   Police work.
   1. Police—Pictorial works. I. Title.
HV8009.F73   363.2   80-22645

ISBN 0-671-25202-X

Acknowledgments

I would like to thank all those who have helped in the making of this book and, in particular, the indispensable people: Lee Jones, Magnum Photos; June Stanier, formerly of the London *Sunday Times Magazine;* Ruth Ansel, *The New York Times Magazine;* and Patrick Bensard of France, who helped with the editing and layout.

Foreword

"A policeman starts out young and impressionable, and you see people at their worst, naturally. You don't get into the better homes, because they have fewer problems, or they keep them under control. Sure, a man and wife argue, but usually it's on a quiet level. In the poorer classes of homes, frustrations are great, pressures are tremendous. So when they have an argument, it's a good argument and it necessitates the police coming to quiet it down. Naturally, the impression of a young police officer is that they aren't really people. . . ."

Tom Kearney's understanding—less rare than may be assumed—has come after "twenty-three hard years" as a cop. In the faces, in the postures, in the world-weariness of Leonard Freed's heroes and heroines are intimations of Tom Kearney's hard-bought wisdom.

Let's face it, the police make up the buffer zone between the haves and the have-nots of our society. A tough young Chicago cop explains it his way: "You created my job, you created me. To you, I'm a robot in uniform. You press a button, and when you call me to the scene you expect results. But I'm also a man. I even have a heart." You may recognize him too in this book.

A young Brooklyn policeman, who works in the emergency service, who experiences horror as his daily fare, reflects on a multi-fatal expressway collision. "The next day I read in the papers they were both boys, but had mod haircuts. You look across the table and you see your son. My wife plenty times asked me, 'How can you do that? How can you go under a train with a person that's got his legs cut off, come home and eat breakfast and feel . . . ?' That's what I'm afraid of, when I can go home and not feel anything for my family. See, I have to feel."

So it is with the men and women whom you casually or studiously observe in this illuminating and strangely moving work. Though they are in uniform, you see beneath their skin.

Studs Terkel

Author's Note

When asked why I became so interested in the police, I have to answer, everyone should be. If we do not concern ourselves with who the police are—who they really are—not just "cops" or "pigs," "law enforcement officers" or "boys in blue," we run the real risk of finding that we no longer have public servants who are required to protect the public, but a lawless army from which we will all take orders. I've seen it as I've worked in countries quite appropriately called "police states."

I was fascinated and challenged by how little people knew about the police, despite the fact that we see them all day in reality and in a fictionalized version at night on TV. I was, and am still, impressed by the concept of the police as a symbol of society's efforts to control itself. And I am as full of questions as any man as to what society should ask of these ordinary persons who, usually to improve their lot, have taken a job which may well require them to kill someone.

I worked alongside and with the police. I "stole" no pictures. When asked if I saw brutality and corruption I have to answer, of course not. But of course there is corruption and brutality, cruelty and callousness. If there were not, then everyone would see the police as angels of mercy and order. What I saw were average people doing a sometimes boring, sometimes corrupting, sometimes dangerous and ugly and unhealthy job. I hope to make people think about who the police are . . . and why we need them.

Leonard Freed

POLICE WORK

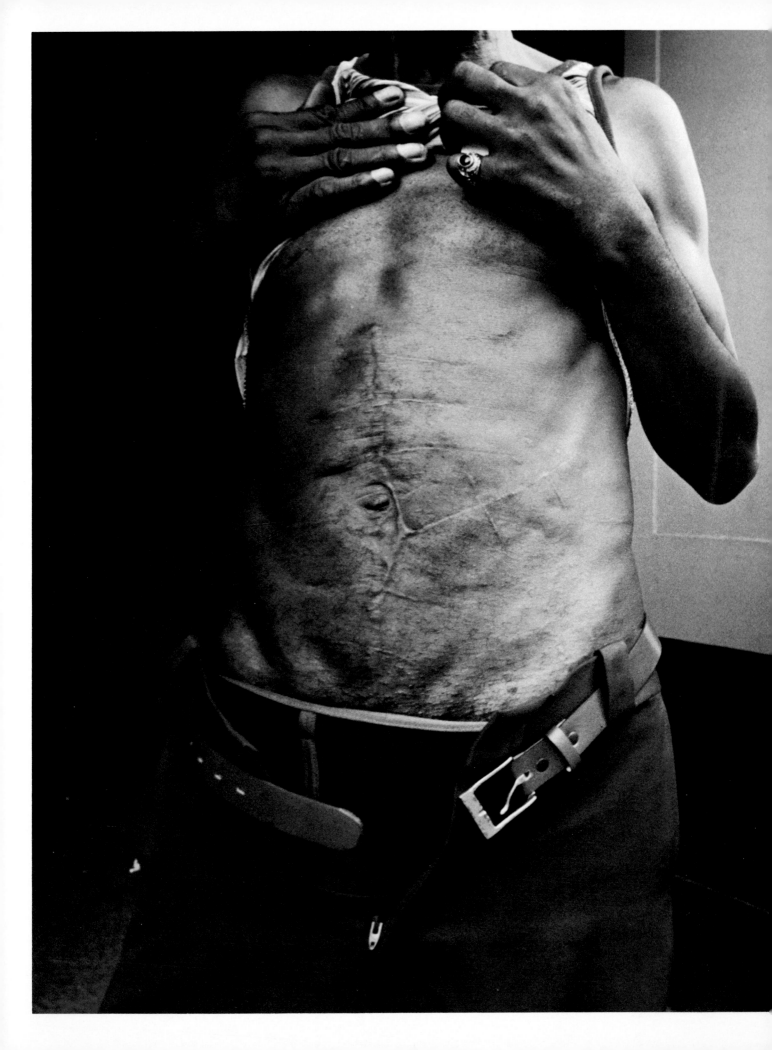

1. The drug pusher showed his knife wounds from past battles. "I'm still alive," he said. "You can never have enough fire power," the officer said.

2. "We're going to pick up a murder suspect," the officer said as he put on a bulletproof vest.

3. "Isn't he cute?" she said.

3

4

6

7

4. New Year's Eve. "Arrest me, arrest me," the man was pleading.

5. The suspect was apprehended. No one paid any attention.

6. A demonstration. Men were called in from all precincts to quell the protesters. The streets filled with the curious. It was an occasion, a social event. People were meeting old friends.

7. Ombudsman.

8. Hired private armies. I could see that most did not have guns, but they were all over, in public and private buildings, in food and clothing stores.

9. Once, alien communities learned to speak the language of the police. Today, good community relations dictate that the police speak the language of the community.

10. Volunteer auxiliary police receive their instructions in the basement of the precinct house. In one police station, I was told, the auxiliaries' lockers had been broken into and parts of uniforms stolen. "Who could have done it?" I asked. "Some cops," the auxiliary said. "Some call us scabs."

9

12

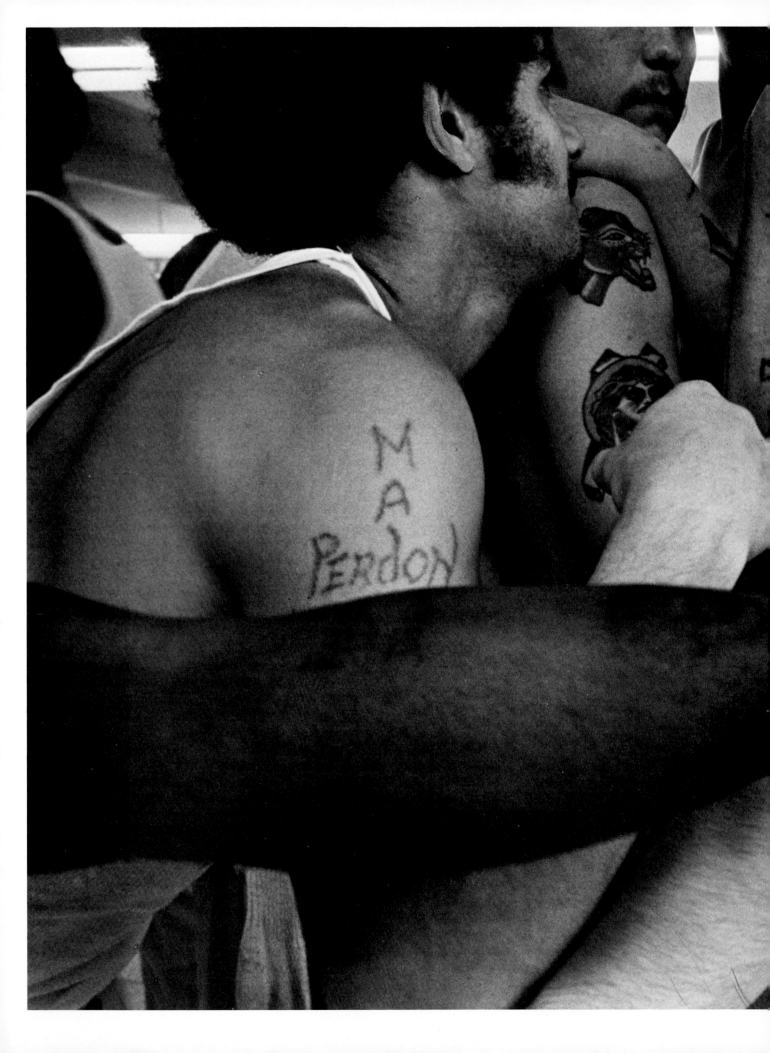

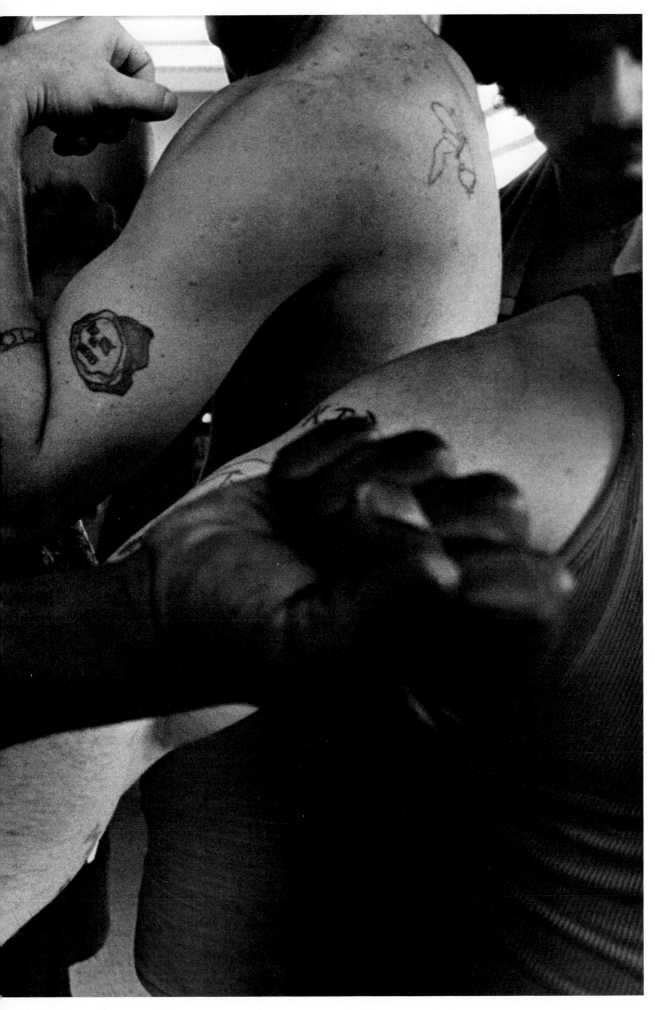

11. The top police brass.

12. Policemen, policewomen.

13. A police officer stationed in a public school tries to spot drug sales to students. "In this school the regular guards are useless," a teacher said. "With us it's real police with real guns stationed in the halls. I'm not a teacher, I'm a warden."

14. At arraignment Polaroid photographs are taken of both the arresting officer and what in official police parlance is called the "alleged perpetrator."

15. The accused and the arresting officer confront each other again in the precinct house.

16. Mostly small-town teenage runaways, still wearing their mothers' lipstick, are picked up at night either by the police or pimps. "These girls in the picture are lucky; the pimps haven't gotten to them yet," said the fatherly officer. "They sleep the night here and in the morning we turn them over to the social workers."

17. "It's a merry-go-round," the officer said. "We pick up the prostitutes, they pay a small fine and are back on the street the same evening. It's just an inconvenience." "Inconvenient to whom?" I asked. "The public," he said. "The public."

18. The girl had been shouting abuse. Now she was handcuffed to a chair in an empty room. An officer looked in and said, "Too hot to handle."

19. The city's house of detention. "What's on this floor?" I asked the guard. "The political prisoners." "You've got a whole floor of political prisoners?" "Yeah, that's what they call themselves. I can't see it—claiming we've taken away their civil rights. I'm black also. To me they're murderers and muggers, just ordinary criminals."

20. House of detention, underground passages.

21. Their arms were notched like a hunter's rifle. "Show me your tattoos," I said to the prisoners. They did. A fight broke out. They were a box of matches ready to go up in flames.

22. Two officers check a suspect auto for a man wanted by the police. They're using the proper police procedure, remaining back of the car, and ready with their guns.

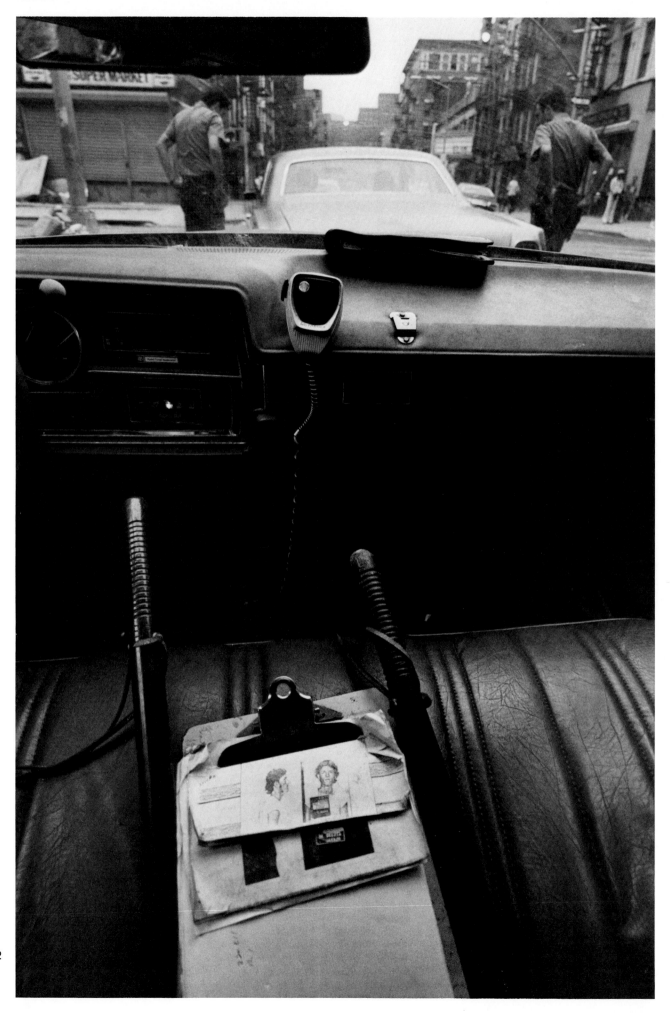

23. "I'll show you how we spend our time," said the homicide investigator, fingering a stack of cards with photos of wanted people. "What we do is mostly paper work. We show the photos in the neighborhood and hope someone will put the finger on a suspect."

24. "There are no pretty girls on my beat. Only the homeless mental patients, the overflow of the social service agencies, the derelicts," said the officer. "The politicians and social workers think if they don't see them, they don't exist. Well, they do exist, and I'm expected to wipe the shit off the streets for them."

25. From a block of abandoned and burned-out buildings, a young girl called to the passing patrol car. She had been raped—gang-banged by her boyfriend's friends while he looked on. As we went to investigate, the neighbors, her girlfriends, screamed "whore" at her. The women tried to tear her clothes off. Did she want the sons and brothers and boyfriends in jail? Calling the cops was, to them, the crime.

26. The police had been called to a tenement upstairs. In the alley, garbage, thrown out of windows, was a banquet for rats.

27. An abandoned building was now a hideaway for derelicts. On a bare mattress lay the body of a man in his mid-thirties. One window was open and the garbage flowed in.

28. Not a bank, but an ordinary grocery store. A burgeoning security industry supplies dogs, fences, alarms and TV surveillance.

29. An officer once said to me that he always worried about his family at home. Who, he wondered, protected them while he worked nights? It made him diligent.

30. Another false alarm. The officers had run up to the top floor, knocked on the door with their guns drawn, only to find a family at dinner, instead of the reported man with a gun. "They do it all the time," the cop said. "They know we must respond to a gun call. It gives them a kick. They stand outside as we run our arse off. It's their idea of a joke."

31. "If I had to, I would shoot," the officer said. "It's best not to think about it. Anyway, most cops never have a reason to shoot in their whole career. Let's hope I'm one of them."

32. Suspects checked for possession of guns.

33. The hotel clerk, the neighbors, his roommate of three years . . . no one knew a thing about the dead young man in the hotel room—not even his real name, or where he worked. The man lay fallen back on the bed, eyes fixed to the ceiling, a hypodermic needle in his arm. "How did this guy die?" I asked the cop. "Dirty drugs." I learned later that he had been a police informer.

34. The neighborhood gathered to watch. Somewhere within the building a man was concealed with a gun.

35. A family argument. When the man went for the woman the police jumped him.

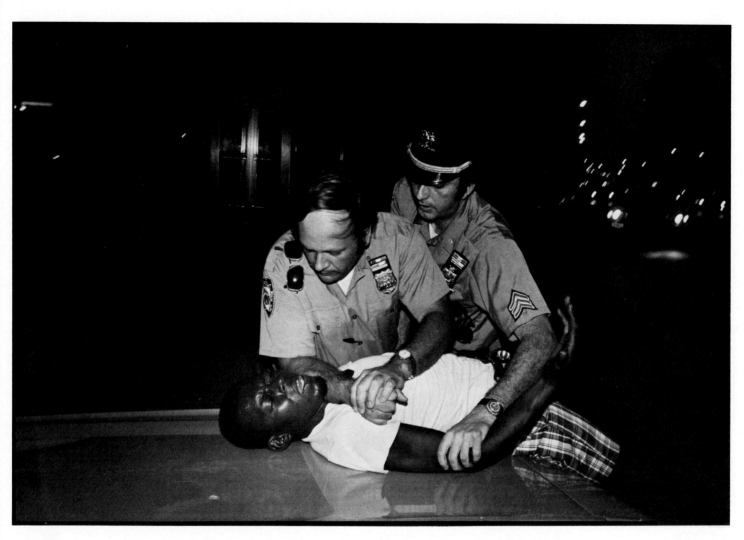

35

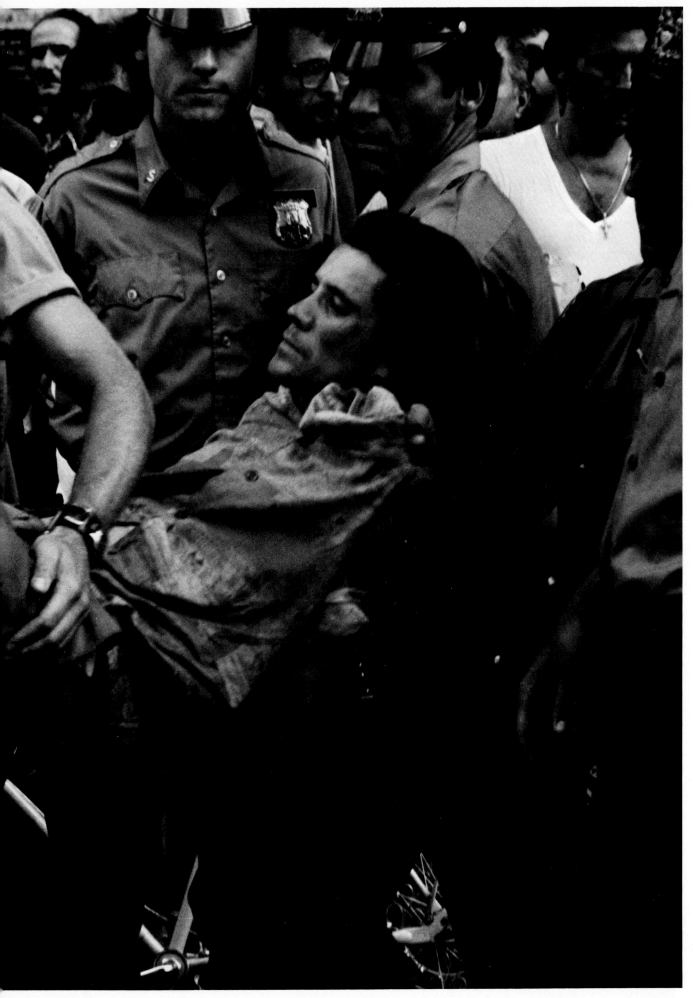

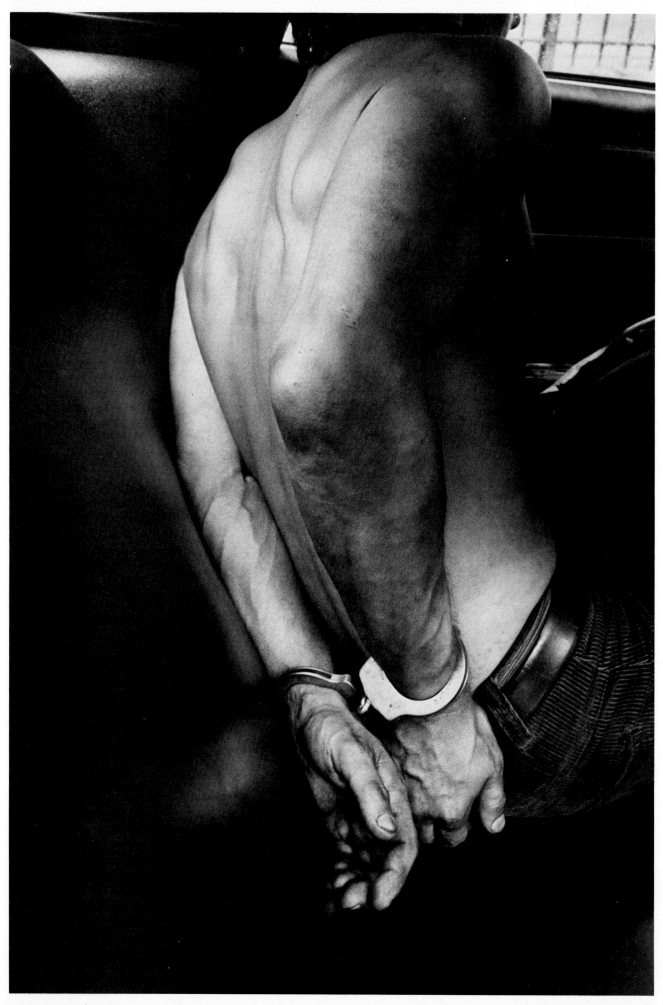

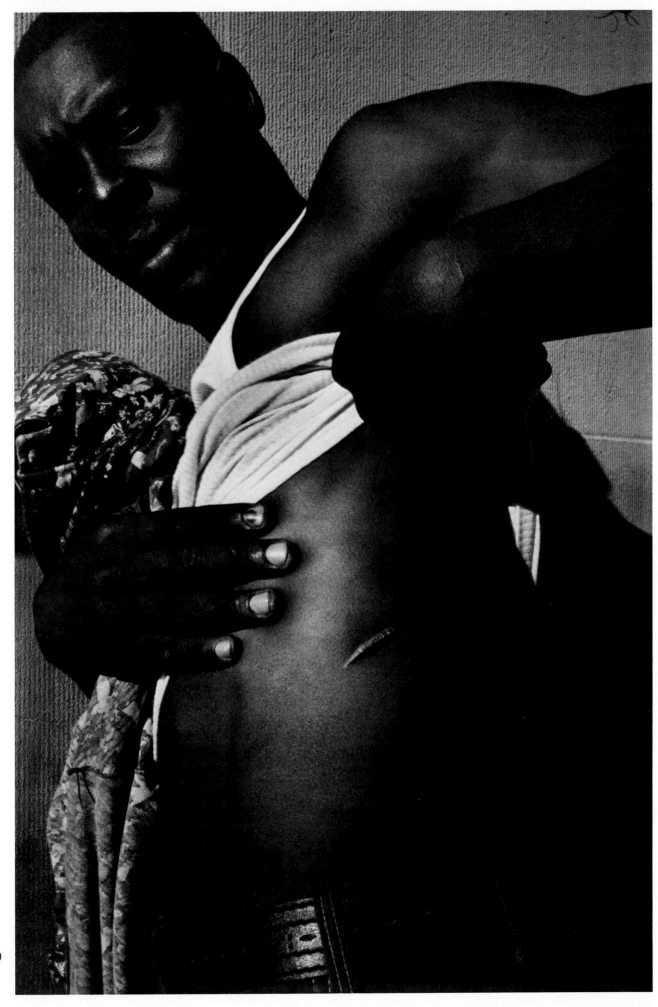

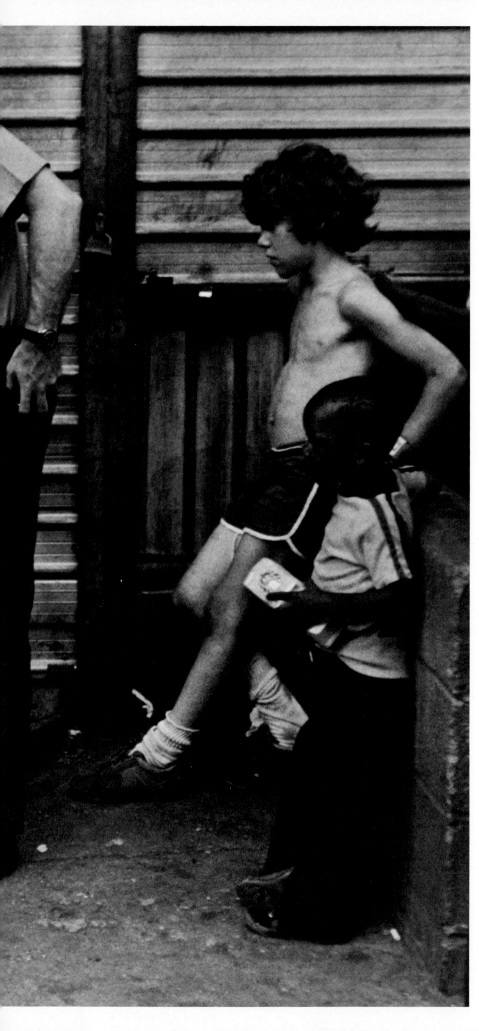

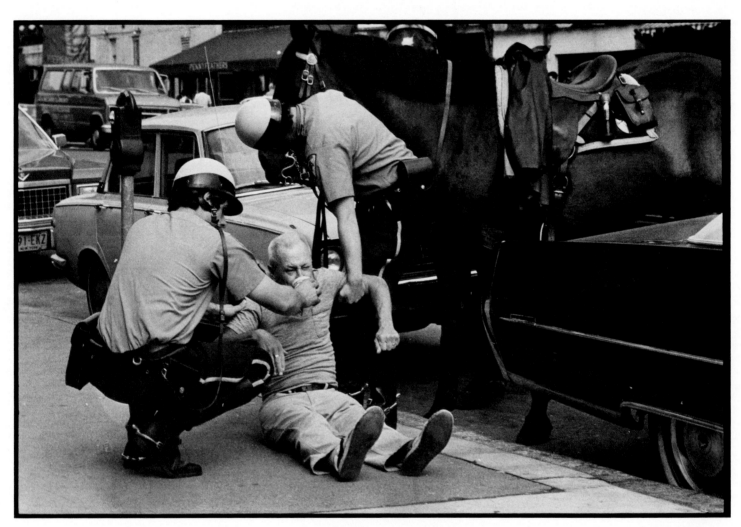

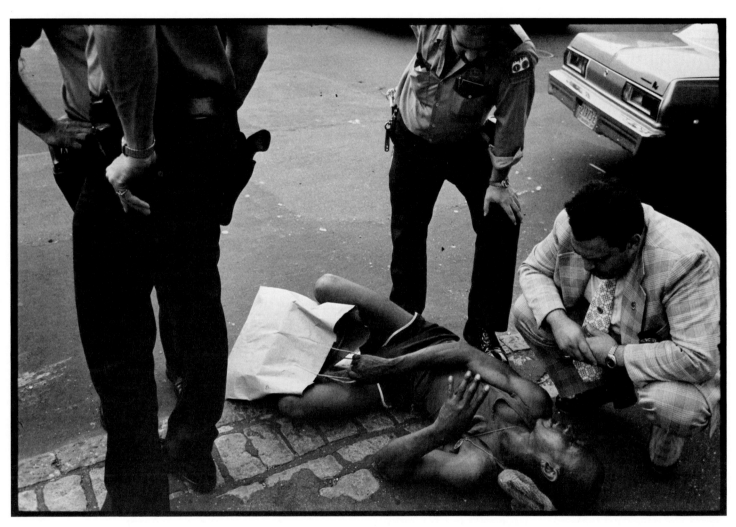

36. A demonstrator refused to stop blocking traffic. The police removed him bodily.

37. Subdued, the man is carried away in a straitjacket.

38. A suspect in the back of a police car.

39. The man showed his wounds from the drug wars. A few weeks later he was knifed again.

40. The man lay unconscious. Someone had placed a note on his chest, suggesting the police be called.

41. Drunk, or sick? An officer inquires.

42. The man was found lying in the street. He will be sent to a hospital. "I don't smoke, but I carry a pack with me. They're useful in such situations," said the officer.

43. Mounted police officers revive a man found unconscious in the street.

44. The police try to sober up a man suspected of taking a drug overdose and get him to a hospital.

45. An officer told me, "I get home after a drunk has spewed all over me and the wife says I stink; she doesn't want me near her. I smell of vomit, shit."

46. The emergency ambulance with a man found on the street.

47. The call coming through the police radio said a woman was seen being dragged, screaming, into an overgrown lot. She was found . . . battered, drugged and unconscious. Though she was known along the street as an addict and a prostitute, all the other pimps and whores said they hadn't seen a thing. The girl later said she hadn't either.

48. The radio call said "street fight." Police and ambulance attendants arrived to find a man unconscious on the pavement.

49. A drug overdose in a hospital emergency room. The doctor said, "Next time it may be too late."

50. The emergency operating room. The woman had been stabbed by her boyfriend. The doctor said, "We save their lives, then get sued for the ugly scars that remain."

51. A hot night on the Bowery. Police try to clear the sidewalk of sleeping drunks.

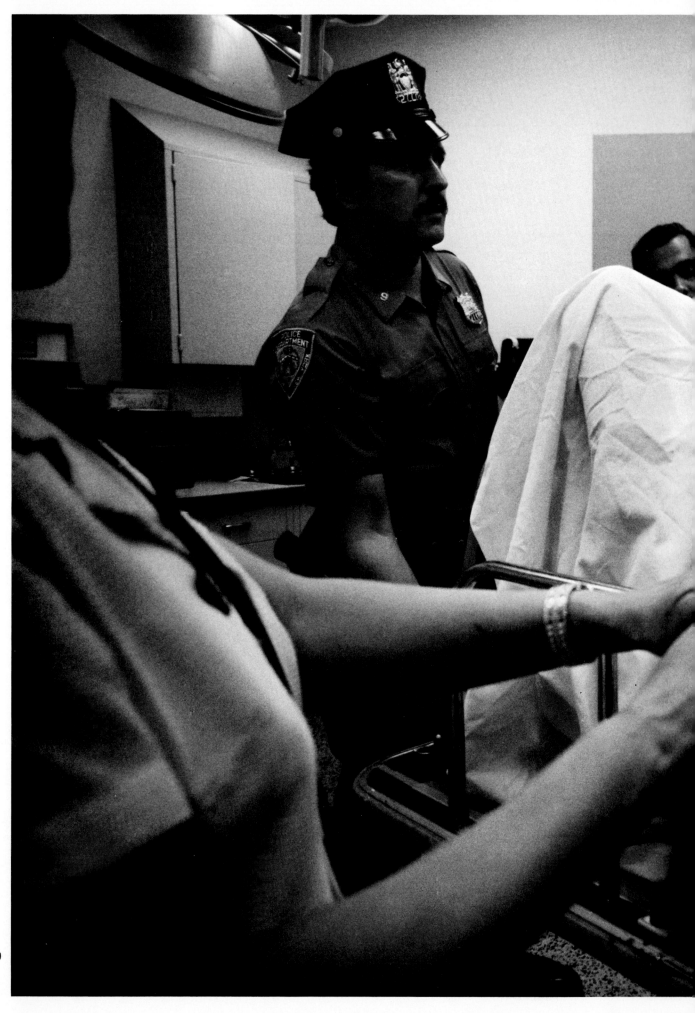

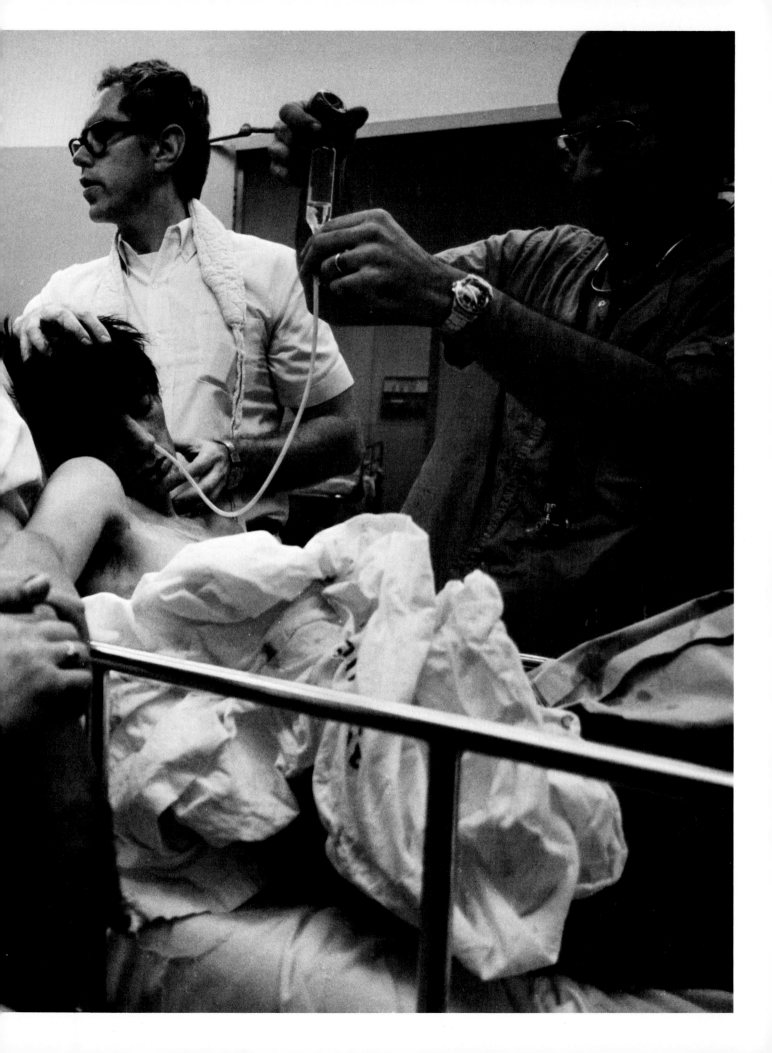

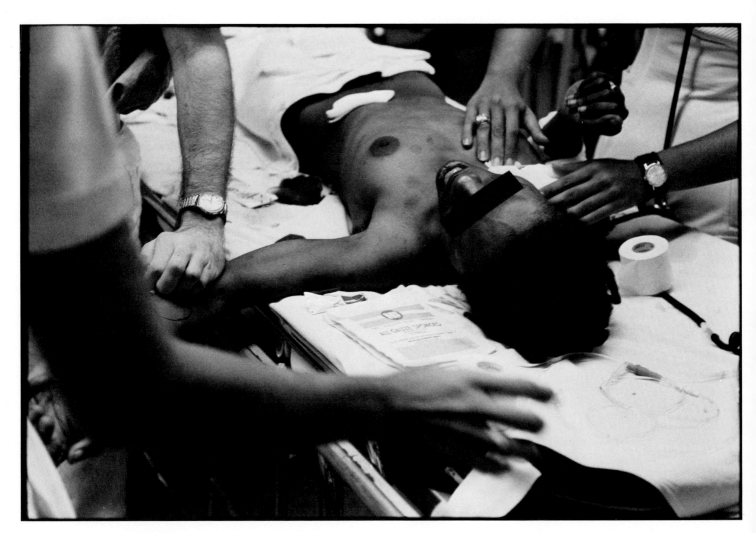

52. It was impossible to tell what had happened. Two women were lying, screaming, on the ground. The street was full of excited people. When the dust cleared we found that a man had been shot. His attacker had escaped in the confusion.

53. Homicide on the living room floor. It was a family affair.

54. Homicide in a food store. The clerk was shot dead for the few dollars in the till.

55. Homicide in a welfare office. On Friday the woman refused to date her former boyfriend. On the weekend he bought a kitchen knife. Monday morning he arrived in the office and again she refused him. He suddenly plunged the knife into her.

56. The police checked out the building. It had no water or heat, but one door had a lock on it. Breaking the lock, they found the dead man.

57. Homicide in the garage of a lavish apartment building. This had all the markings of a Mafia killing. It was explained to me that the Mafia hires skilled lawyers to advise on such things. The man had been shot three times in the back of the head. In order to convict, the state would have to find the three guns, the three men who did the killing, and then prove which of the three bullets actually killed the man, and who fired which gun.

58. The tenants said that the smell in the last few hot summer days had filled the hall. One choked on it, and the heart sank at the thought of entering the apartment. The leakage of the body fluids had soaked the mattress, and the extremities dripped like candles. Maggots had eaten the face away.

59. Dead by drug overdose. The officer said. "Drug-related deaths are hard to solve. With drugs one never knows." Dirty drugs are a lethal weapon.

60. As they pulled him out of the river I could see that his face was gone. He had been in about two weeks.

61. Homicide by drowning. The young man now in the inner room of the city morgue, where all decomposed bodies are investigated, had been found handcuffed, nude and submerged in a bathtub.

62. Homicide detectives produce fingerprints from a corpse in the city morgue.

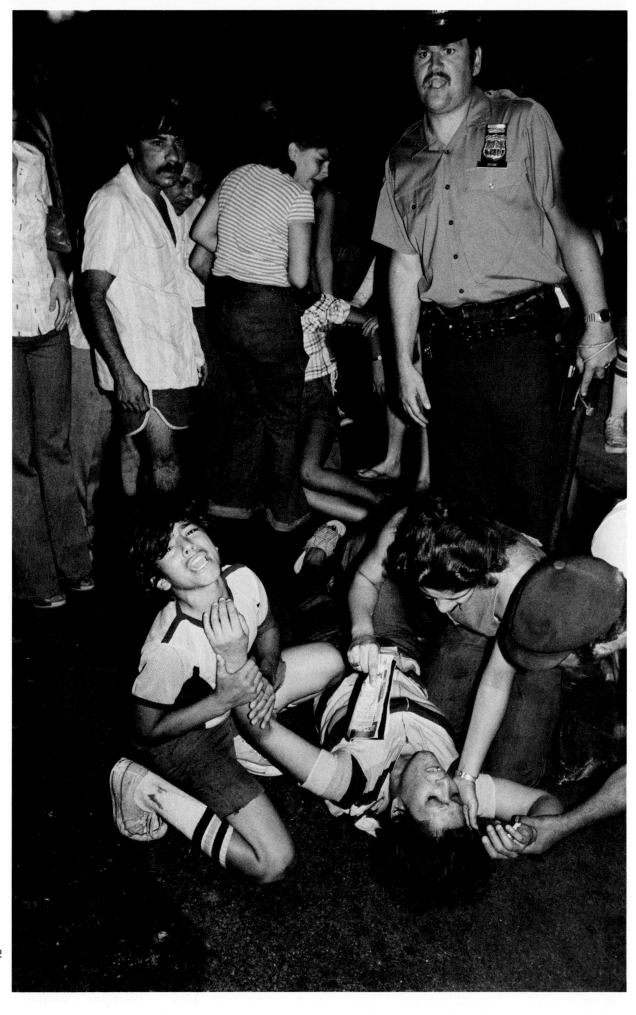

52

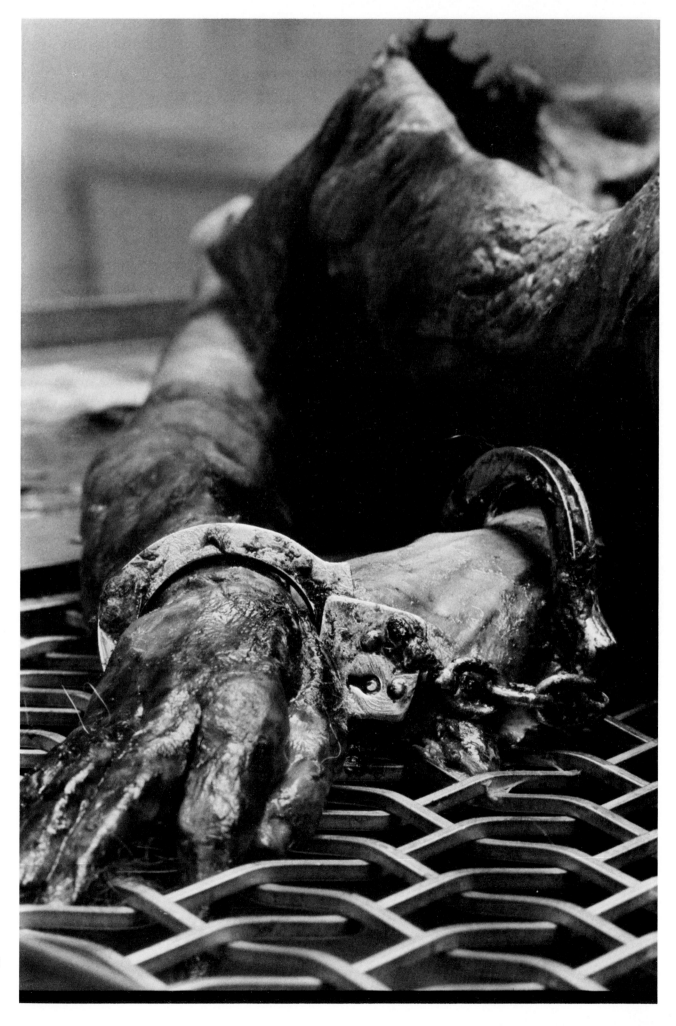

66

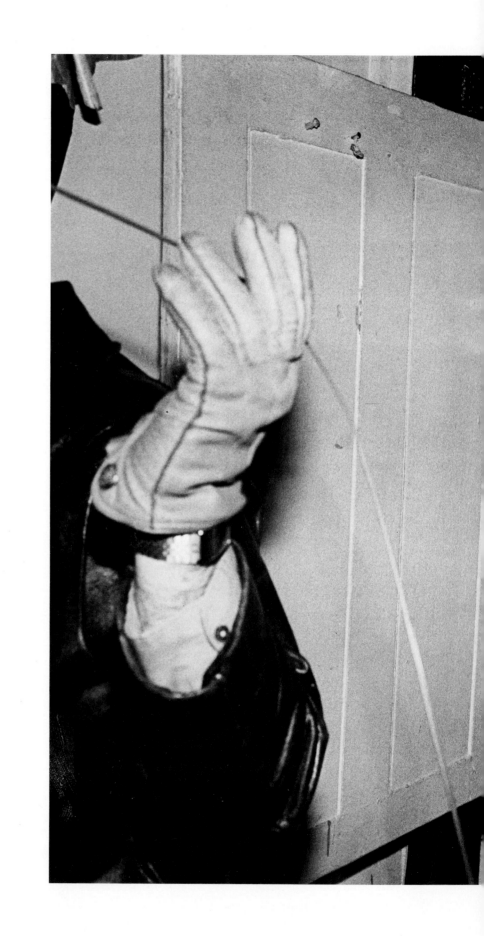

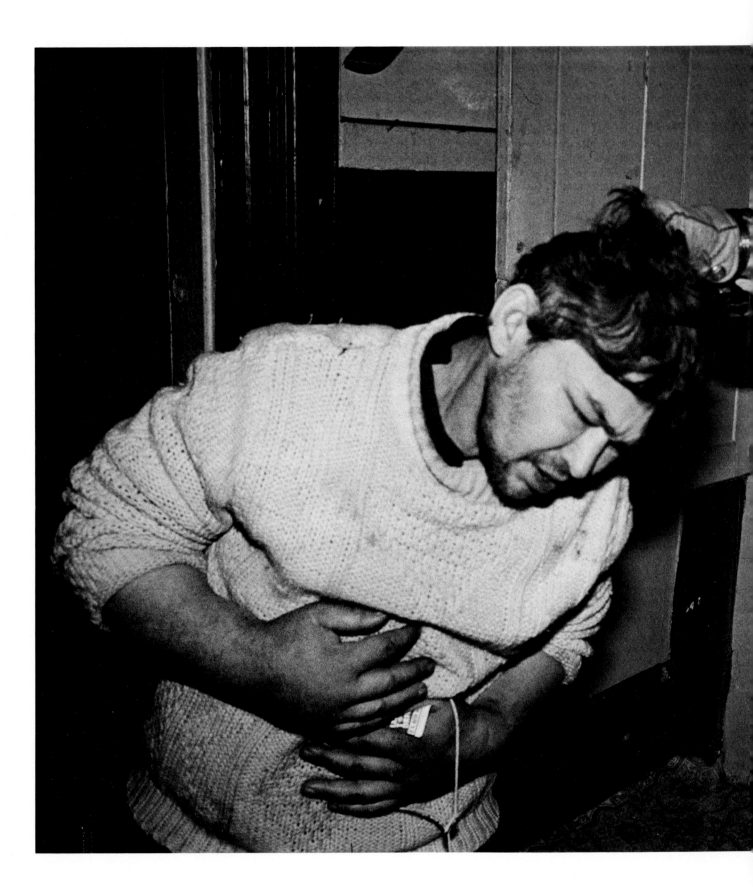

63. An abandoned building. Inside, the officer found a "shooting gallery," where drug addicts go to buy dreams or to die.

64. Caught in the hallway of the abandoned building, a junkie is searched for drugs. Seconds before, on seeing the police, he had turned, dashed up the stairs, scattering everything from his pockets as he went.

65. The "shooting gallery." The police pulled out the illegal wiring connected to the street lights, smashed windows. The officer said, "All we do is inconvenience them, destroy some drugs. Nothing changes."

66. The raid, a big one, had about a dozen undercover men. The police were armed with battering rams and hydraulic drills to force their way into the fortress-like apartment, with its steel doors and frames. They were confident they would get some of the bigger boys in this drug distribution center for the "shooting galleries." What they did get were boxes of packaged drugs and a woman who, the police said, would be free that evening on bail. Through the window I could see the pushers watching and waiting for the police to leave.

67. "Shooting gallery" lavatory clogged with gelatine capsules and syringes.

68. "Shooting gallery" tables, with syringes.

69–71. The "shooting gallery" raid was over and the officers were leaving when from the back room an officer called for us to return. He had found something. Crouched and terrified in a closet was an addict, tourniquet on his upper arm, holding a syringe in his hand.

72. In the police headquarters photo identification sector. The machine makes a composite photo from various human head characteristics.

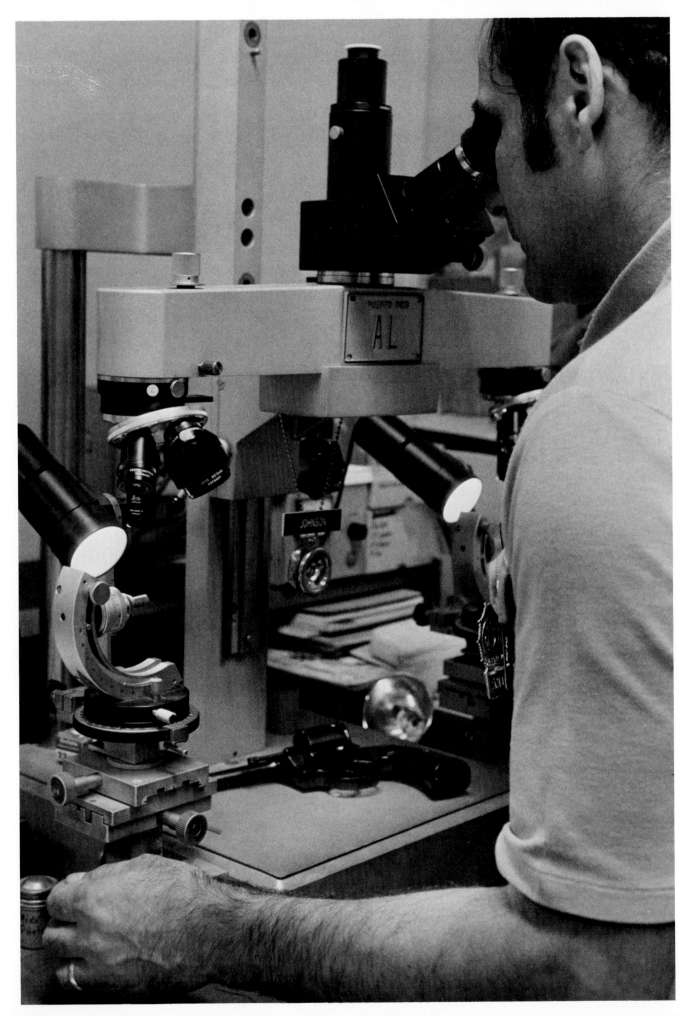

76

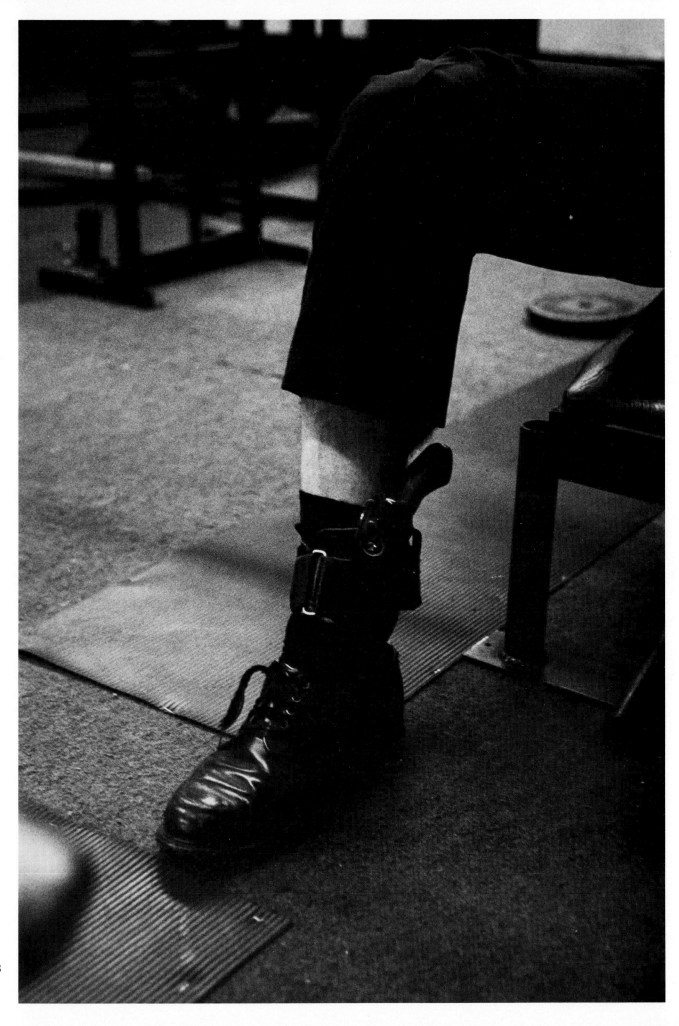

73. In the final analysis, fingerprint identification must be done by an experienced eye.

74. Working with a witness, a police artist draws a composite of a suspect.

75. A bullet expert in the police forensic sector studies the marking on a spent bullet.

76. The curator of the police museum holds a trophy out of the "romantic" epoch of gang warfare.

77. A bullet test by a forensic expert.

78. Police officers have built a gym for themselves. They use it mostly during lunch breaks, and often have no time to change clothes or remove their ankle revolvers.

79. The gym.

80. Police academy baton and judo training by male and female police recruits.

81. Before a tour of duty.

82. Frogmen.

85

89

93

94

83. A precinct detective squad.

84. Homicide detectives working around the clock on a double cop-killing case. The detective said, "We're working this case on our own time."

85. Paper work. Everything is written down.

86. In the back room of the precinct house. Officers register their prisoners.

87. A detective registers rifles confiscated in a police raid.

88. Quiet times at the station. An officer sweeps up. A woman police volunteer takes calls.

89. Two A.M. More paper work.

90. The burglar, caught in the process of breaking through a brick wall between one shop and another, asked that the tools of his trade be returned to him.

91. A foot patrol officer drops in to chat with a neighborhood theatrical group.

92. Trendy, looking tough, but only pussycats.

93. Police officers visit a counterculture dress boutique.

94. Police presence. Most foot patrol is standing and watching.

95. A police officer relaxes for a moment at a street festival.

96. A community group accuses a precinct of maltreating a suspect.

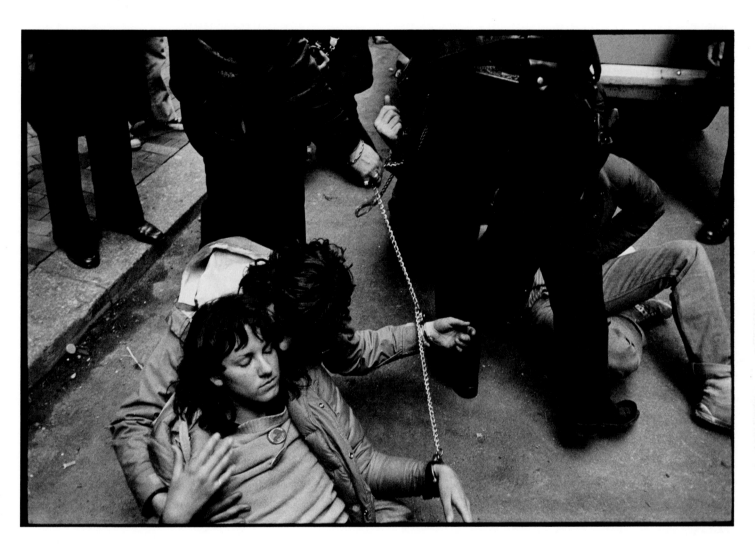

103

104

97. A massive round-the-clock show of force by the police to protect a foreign head of state from his own countrymen.

98. Demonstrators are arrested for obstructing traffic.

99. Over the years, police and demonstrators have worked out a compromise. A bit of pushing and bruising is permitted, but not too much.

100. The police rushed to the supermarket after a call said a holdup was in progress, and caught a teenager running from the scene. The store manager said they'd caught the wrong person. Later, a police check showed he was suspected of other crimes.

101. Youngsters fighting in the street are separated by police officers.

102. A young boy who says he has been left alone comes to the precinct station house for help. A concerned neighbor looks on.

103. A suspect resisting arrest.

104. A young man explains to police how the car was wrecked.

105. On a warm July day neighborhood children play in a patrol car. At another time, an officer reminisced about wintry midnight tours, about the isolation he felt in the patrol car. Night after night he drove the same streets, saw the same drunks, homeless ones, addicts, whom he had to move on, clearing the street. He had his anxieties. What, he wondered, would he do if one night they were gone? Whom would he talk to?

106. Halloween. A young man dressed as an angel seeks a ride in a patrol car.

107. Police scooter patrol.

108. A policewoman plays games with community children. Shortly afterward, the officer became pregnant and was assigned a desk job for the period of her pregnancy.

109. A police officer and his bride in the church before their wedding.

110. Christmas. A policeman, his family and a neighborhood friend in the basement playroom of their house.

111. Christmas. An officer and his wife at home.

112. A police officer and family pose in their fishing boat, parked in their yard.

113. Another police family pose in their backyard swimming pool. Their house is in the background.

114, 115. A police patrol car team: He is a Civil War buff on his off hours, and poses here in authentic Civil War gear, with his children in the basement of his home. She is a mother of two and a cycle enthusiast.

116-120. A funeral for an officer killed in the line of duty.

116

118

121. The police line breaks up after the passing of a foreign dignitary.

122. A police officer at his post during the filming of a movie. There is a growing "police cult"; aficionados wear the odds and ends of uniforms, swagger along the street with handcuffs, keys and whistles dangling from their belts.

122

123. Central booking at night. An officer entertains with a puppet show. The puppet shoots those who do not give satisfactory answers to his "questions."

124. A police officer patiently waits in the hospital emergency ward for a victim, shot in the leg, to say what happened.

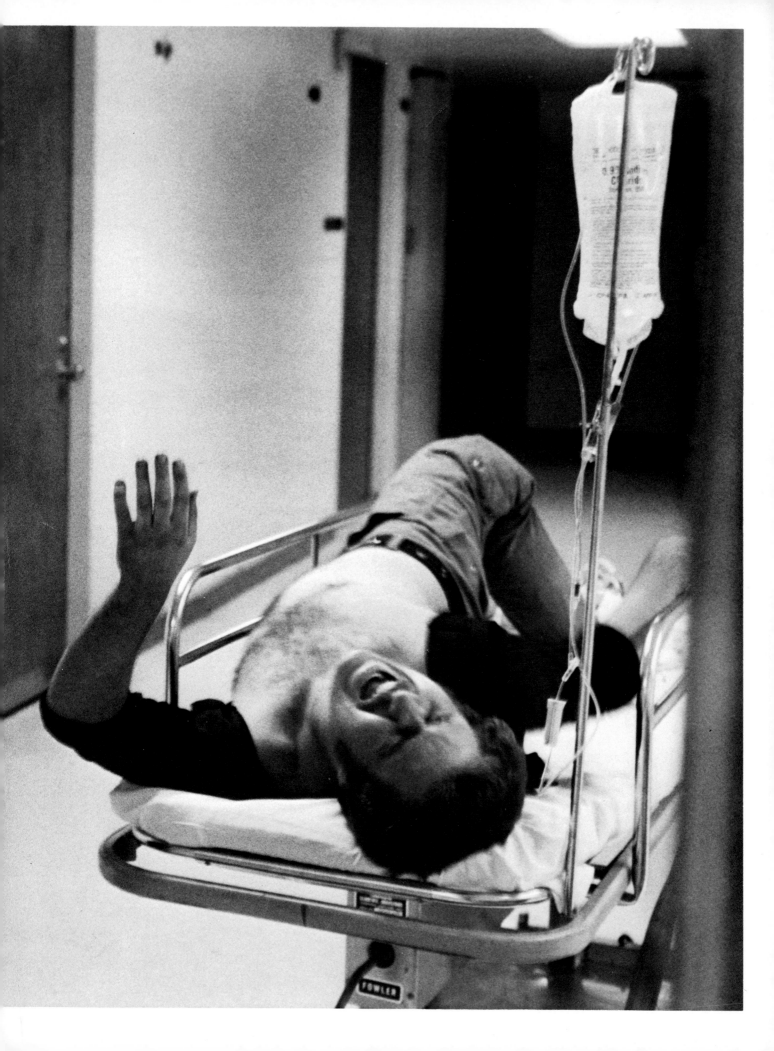

About the Author

Leonard Freed is a world-renowned photo-journalist and art photographer. He has exhibited in New York, Paris, and Amsterdam. His books include *Black in White America, Made in Germany,* and *Berlin.*

Leonard Freed's work has appeared in *Life, Look,* and other international magazines.